First published in Great Britain 1984 by Colour Library Books Ltd.
© 1984 Illustrations: London Features International Ltd.,
    Joe Bangay Photography Ltd., and Jill Furmanovsky.
© 1984 Text: Colour Library Books Ltd., Guildford, Surrey, England.
Colour separations by Reprocolor Llovet, S.A., Barcelona, Spain.
Printed and bound by Rieusset, S.A. in Barcelona, Spain.
ISBN 0 86283 189 X

BOY GEORGE

and CULTURE CLUB

Maria David

Produced by
Ted Smart
and
Gerald Hughes

Edited by
David Gibbon

Designed by
Philip Clucas MSIAD

COLOUR LIBRARY BOOKS

"I wasn't born with any special magic. I got bored and picked on and beaten up at school. Sometimes I've got a spotty skin or double chin or I feel sick."

So says George Alan O'Dowd, with that wry candour that so disarms even those who want to disapprove of him. The thing that makes George – you know, *that* George, *the* George, outrageous, ambiguous, million-selling Boy George – so lovable is that underneath the raggedy-man camp and the perfectly painted lips, he's so damned normal.

For the last fifteen years at least, the music business (and, of course, the nation's newspapers) has been desperately searching for something to tag "the new Beatles". In their search for something as youthful, talented and universally appealing as those Sixties icons, they can hardly be blamed for overlooking the said George Alan, as he worked his way inexorably from night-club poseur to world-wide pop phenomenon. Yet here he

is, having crept up on them from behind – Boy George, not the freak, not the transvestite, not the affected mannequin, but the one pop star your mum would like to drop in for tea and even your granny has heard about.

Sure, George is glamorous, but he's *comfortable* with it. Certainly, he conforms to none of the stereotypes of masculinity, but then he's one of the stars who doesn't sell himself on his sexuality. So he threatens no-one. His message to the little girls who worship him isn't "Come to bed with me". He doesn't urge their brothers "Be gay". When he exclaimed to a women's magazine, "Sex? I'd rather have a nice cup of tea!" a thousand housewifely heads must have nodded in agreement.

Boy George's appearance isn't a symptom of anything, beyond an openness to the influence of any colourful, cultural thing he sees around him. Hassidic Jew's hat, Japanese kimono, Romany emblems or nun's habit, it's all the same to George.

Put them together and what have you got? "Don't judge a book by its cover", says George, and he's right, you'd better not try. A whole convention of shrinks could go barmy in the attempt.

George was born on June 14th, 1961 in Bexley Hospital, the third child of Jeremiah and Diana O'Dowd. He grew up in Eltham, South East London; dad was a builder and mum a harassed housewife, trying to manage a growing brood that eventually settled at five sons and a daughter.

The family were Catholic, and in George's early days church on Sunday was an unavoidable ritual. Then one day, George recalls, "My little brother took his trousers down in church, so we never went back again. I was very pleased about that."

Schooldays were a difficult time for George, though probably more difficult for his teachers and long-suffering parents. Even in his early teens, he'd be blithely over-the-top in appearance, showing up for

school (when he bothered to show up) in gigantic platform shoes and sporting a bright orange Ziggy Stardust-style haircut.

Eltham Green School was definitely not ready for this apparition. Truanting, cheeky and unable to be convinced that being *In Charge* meant being *In The Right*, George was banished to a class of "problem" kids, nicknamed *The Greenhouse*. But not even the Special Needs Department, to give it its correct name, could contain our hero.

In September 1976, a letter from the headmaster, Peter Dawson, told Mr and Mrs O'Dowd that George was to be suspended from school. It requested that both of them attend a meeting with the head, and tellingly added that several copies of the letter were being sent to them via various channels, since the one given to George to take home was unlikely to reach its destination!

That was end of George's school career. Anyway, he had more interesting things to do. By now he was a regular frequenter of the wilder sort of night clubs, and in those days before punk or the glittering "new romantics", that meant the gay clubs.

There was Bangs, Visuals, Chaguarama's (try saying it) and more. Punk arrived, and clubs like the Roxy sprang up. He went to those, too, did a brief stint as a sales assistant in a Kings Road clothes shop and an even briefer one at Tesco's supermarket, then jacked the whole thing in and went to live in

Birmingham for a year.

"I remember George from our early gigs," says Dave Wakeling, then lead singer with The Beat. "At that time, nearly everyone *except* him was pretending to be a big pop star."

Not that George had toned himself down. "I got on with everyone because I had such a big mouth," he recalls. "My hair was mauve and I used to go out with a green face, or a blue face and a red neck."

His return to London was a typically timely move. Tired of the harsh music and pseudo-political attitudes of punk, a clique of London club-goers was creating its own little scene; a throw-back to early Seventies glam-rock but with added camp, a no-holds barred party where you could do anything at all except come as you are.

They pinched a lot of their sartorial style from the various phases of David Bowie's career – moonman, Ziggy, the silver-painted Aladdin Sane, the baggy-trousered soulie – and the music they danced to was derived from his electronic albums.

The whole thing began with a weekly 'Bowie Night' at Billy's, a tiny Soho nightspot, hosted by Rusty Egan and Steve Strange. Egan was a pop drummer turned DJ-cum-entrepreneur, a monumentally mouthy barrow boy who ran the business side and played the narrow selection of electro-dance music – mostly old Roxy Music, Kraftwerk and, of course, Bowie.

Strange, a Welsh boy who'd arrived in

London with punk and hung around with most of its stars, was the club's greeter – or rather selector. Attired in some outlandish garb, he would stand guard at the door and only grant admittance to those who looked *right* – like the bride of Dracula, say, or a character from a low-budget sci-fi film.

Nothing could have suited George better than this environment – a mini-society of aspiring fashion designers, musicians, hairdressers and poseurs; a bitchy microcosm where style was all and the everyday world was refused entry.

In 1980, the Strange-Egan club night moved to Hell, and thence to the Blitz, a larger venue. But the strict admittance policy remained, though it was no problem to George, who managed to cause a stir even amongst his outrageous peers by turning up dressed as a nun. Robed in white, with wimple and crucifix, he told the street-wise style magazine I-D, "I'm a budding celebrity, the immaculate conception."

The "Blitz Kids", as they became known, or the "New Romantics", to give them another title they all loathed, were scoffed at by many as superficial nancy-boys who couldn't hope to rival the recently-departed punk explosion in terms of music, fashion and style ideas. But a surprising number of talented individuals can be traced back to those early club days, though most of them wouldn't thank you for exhuming the pictures of them in their frilly shirts and knickerbockers.

Until George's recent runaway success as a pop star, Spandau Ballet were the biggest musical success to come out of the Blitz. They used the elitism of the club scene to launch themselves into a lucrative record company deal, and inspired many of their Blitz contemporaries (George included, probably) to have a go. Steve Strange and Rusty Egan roped in a clutch of light-heavyweight musician friends to form Visage, and with 'Fade to Grey' scored an instant hit. As the chap in the high street, or at least his girfriend, began to adopt a watered-down Blitz Kid look, the Visage LP became an international best-seller.

Stephen Linard, another face of the time, is now a top clothes designer based in Japan, while Kirk Brandon, extremely close friend to George in those days, has scored a measure of success with his bands Theatre Of Hate and Spear Of Destiny.

Jeremy Healey, a schoolfriend of George's later named himself Jeremiah (after George's dad) and became half of the notorious duo Haysi Fantayzee. Marilyn, George's one-time comrade in arms (they both lived in a squat in Carburton Street) used to appear in total Monroe drag, massive masculine shoulders bursting from a tiny black cocktail frock. Now he's a pop star himself, trying hard to move out of the Boy's shadow, and the two aren't on speaking terms.

But to return to George – who by now had more-or-less lost his surname. If you mentioned him in those days and anyone asked you "Who?", you'd say "You know, *George*!" and, provided the questioner had the least clue about what was happening in London, he'd know. George was the real

face of the Blitz scene; Steve Strange might be making the Fleet Street papers, but George was younger, brighter, prettier. And cheekier. At a Spandau Ballet concert, photographers queueing to snap the freakily-dressed audience were charged 50p a pose by George. It bought him his drinks for the whole evening.

He appeared on the cover of various glossy European magazines, and was on the books of the Peter Benison model agency – "It's our new, weirdo side," they explained. He popped up in an ad for the Trustee Savings Bank, and a TV commercial for British Airways.

"In it I'm walking into Stringfellow's when this 'plane flies overhead and I look up at it," he enthused at the time. "They showed it on TV on the day of the Royal

Wedding – my mum was really pleased!"

George was a minor celebrity, albeit only to the scene-makers and media folk in the capital. But now came two separate chances to exploit his flamboyant personality – one in music, and one in fashion.

Malcolm McLaren, the svengali who created the Sex Pistols, had gone on to work with Adam And The Ants. He sold Adam the idea of a pirate look and a Burundi drum beat, then walked out, taking the Ants with him. He then presented them with one Annabella Lwin, a beautiful 14-year-old half-Burmese Saturday girl from his local dry cleaners. She was to be their new lead singer!

With McLaren pulling the strings, the group came up with some raw but

brilliantly exciting records and a terrific pirate image – the clothes all came from Worlds End, the Kings Road shop run by McLaren's partner Viv Westwood, the originator of that pirate look. But the group were unhappy with Annabella. She wasn't pulling her weight, they said. She needed bucking up a bit. And that's where George came in.

Bow Wow Wow's guitarist, Matthew Ashman, had a girlfriend called Gabriella who worked at the Benison agency. She introduced him to George, and Matthew began lobbying the rest of the group for George to join. The devious McLaren declared that the "Wowsers", as they called themselves, were to have a new, joint lead singer to augment Annabella's youthful presence. The character was to be called Lieutenant Lush, and George was to play him.

He made his debut at Bow Wow Wow's headlining concert at the Rainbow Theatre, Finsbury Park, North London. All the downstairs seats had been taken out and a small funfair installed, with game stalls and even a full-size helter-skelter – all part of McLaren's kiddie fun image for the group.

Their usual set over, they appeared for an encore with George on lead vocals. Though most of the audience didn't know who he was, he went down very well, and subsequent reviews in the music press were more than kind, not to say intrigued. But George, with his determined ideas and quick tongue, soon fell into disagreement with Malcolm McLaren. Besides, the very much more docile Annabella, fearing that she was about to be replaced altogether by the Lieutenant, pulled her socks up. After a couple more gigs together, George and the Wowsers went their separate ways.

George later maintained, however, that many of the ideas for the lyrics of their first LP, the exhaustingly-titled 'See Jungle! See Jungle! Go Join Your Gang, Yeah! City All Over, Go Ape Crazy!' were his.

George's friend Phillip Sallon, from whom he later rented his St John's Wood flat, proved a useful connection more than once in those days. An unbelievably over-the-top character who'd been around since the first days of punk and now ran the pirate-dressers club Planets, Sallon had a father who, usefully enough, worked on one of the Fleet Street tabloids. When a "New outrageous, fashions, can't tell the boys from the girls" – type feature was required, George was called in to model.

Phillip had a day job in the wardrobe department at the Opera in Covent Garden, and George, too, ventured briefly into the world of the theatre, working as a stylist on a play called 'Naked Robots', put on by the Royal Shakespeare Company.

"I used to be so rough with the actors," he says. "Like a footballer. And I made all the women look like drag queens. They hated it, but I like drag queens."

Costumes were supplied by a shop called Street Theatre. George got on well with the proprietor, Peter Small, and took to dressing his shop windows for him – not just in Street Theatre, which sold interesting clothes by young designers and a great deal of shoddy New Romantic tat, but for its sister shop over the road, The Regal, which specialised in Sixties-style psychedelic gear.

Peter Small offered George his second big career opportunity – to run his own shop, just round the corner in Ganton Street, a little turning off Carnaby Street. George took it on and christened it The Foundry. He came up with the ideas for many of the clothes in the shop, overseeing their make-up by frequent visits to the tiny workshop nearby where they were put together.

The Foundry sold mock-taffeta dresses with huge leg o'mutton sleeves, baggy trousers, wide painted ties, wildly colourful

shirts, and a rather amusing line in dress shirts that were transparent but for a modesty-preserving front panel. George was not to be seen sporting those, though he did go out once or twice in a roomy zoot suit, when the craze for those was upon us.

"But August Darnell from Kid Creole And The Coconuts is the only man in the world who really looks good in these," he observed ruefully.

Above all, though, the Foundry made its name on the clothes of Sue Clowes. Basically a fabric rather than a clothes designer, she came up with a style of prints that perfectly reflected George's grab-bag style – a mishmash of cultural bits and pieces that included roses, aeroplanes, Romany hieroglyphics and the Star of David. They turned out tee-shirts, cropped trousers and white cotton shifts emblazoned with those stunning Clowes prints – and so, almost before Culture Club, the Culture Club look was born.

George had resolved to form his own group after his career with Bow Wow Wow was stillborn. He'd always had a good voice – chatting breathlessly in some sweaty club, he'd surprise you by singing a line from some old soul song he'd been talking about, in a sweet and tuneful voice.

A mutual friend introduced him to bass player Mikey Craig at Planets, where George and a friend called Dancing Dick shared DJ duties. They enlisted a guitarist called Suede, and set about looking for a drummer.

At this time they were calling themselves the Sex Gang Children, after a line in a Bow Wow Wow song called 'Mile High Club'. The song's content, a tale of animals transported in inhumane conditions on board an aeroplane, is sufficiently offbeat to suggest that George may have been involved in writing it. Certainly the original version began, "This is your Captain Lush speaking…"

George's friend Kirk Brandon suggested to the trio that they get hold of Jon Moss. Jon had drummed with most of the punk bands worth mentioning, but more recently had packed up the music business in a mood of disillusionment and was working for a video company. He hit it off with George straight away, though, and joined the band – on one condition: the name had to go.

Eventually they agreed on Culture Club. (Another young group later asked George if they could use the old name, and so the Sex Gang Children [no relation] were named.) Suede, the guitarist, was sacked, to make way for Roy Hay. The Club had been set up.

Culture Club were determined not to fall into the trap that had spiked many of their friends; that of trying to sell themselves on image alone before they'd got their music properly together. After months of rehearsal, they played their first gigs in the autumn of 1981. By new year, the record companies came looking for them.

Even though the first demo recordings they produced were less than brilliant, Culture Club had the striking image and enough promise of musical talent to get themselves signed to a major label pretty quickly. Mostly, of course, they had George, a front-man with bags of personality and a look that grabbed instant attention from everyone.

After talking with several companies, they eventually signed to Virgin Records because they liked the friendly enthusiasm of the people there. In May 1982, their first single, 'White Boy', was released, followed only a month later by their second, 'I'm Afraid Of Me'. Neither was a hit, and George, volatile as ever, was downcast.

But the third, 'Do You Really Want To

Hurt Me', released in September, was the turning point, a lilting blend of pop and lovers'-rock, the gentle side of reggae, it impressed everyone from the critics on the music papers to the people at Radio 2, who made it Record Of The Week.

In November, 1982 the band appeared on Top Of The Pops for the first time. George skipped and sang and charmed and, predictably, shocked a few people. Quite a lot of mums and dads, however, seemed to be under the impression that he was a girl anyway...

The record went to Number One, and the newspapers began their fascination with Boy George. "The Gender Bender!" they dubbed him, and plenty more foolish things besides.

"It's like childbirth when you get to Number One, the relief and the ecstasy," said George, adding with his usual common sense, "but then you stop thinking about it. If it rules your life for the next five years, there's something wrong with you."

The British number one slot was just the beginning, though. 'Do You Really Want To Hurt Me' became a Number One all over the world, even conquering the American charts. Many people thought that George's look would prevent him from being really big in the USA, where tastes tend to be a little more conservative. But the song was so strong, there was no stopping it.

"Our music is very traditional," George points out. "You don't have to sit back and go oooh, isn't it weird... One thing Jon pointed out about America was when we played there, they listened to my singing and when it came to a part of the song they liked, they'd clap. I'm a *singer* there, not just freaky George."

The group has always endeavoured to put themselves forward as an entity, not, in George's words, "gorgeous glossy George and the three odd bods behind him".

The follow-up to their first hit was 'Time (Clock Of The Heart)', a gorgeous soulful song that was very different from 'Do You Really'. It was, as one reviewer pointed out, a song that Smokey Robinson might be proud to have written, and it confirmed that Culture Club were much more than well-dressed, one-hit wonders.

George was voted Pop Personality of the Year by Daily Mirror readers in the Mirror/BBC Rock And Pop Awards, a title he held onto the following year. The only group that came close to rivalling Culture Club in popularity was Duran Duran, but theirs is very much a young-girl audience. They are pin-ups to the little girls, but George wins the mums and dads round as well, and in the end that's sure to establish him beyond reasonable doubt as the world's top pop star.

All through 1983, the success story rampaged on. George, who'd never left England before joining the group, found himself away from home most of the time, touring around the world.

"I hated the travelling at first," he says. "I never wanted to leave England. Now it's like using the bus, and I still hate it."

'Church Of The Poison Mind', a stomping, Tamla-Motown style song, continued their trail of hit singles and followed on the success of the debut LP, 'Kissing To Be Clever'.

But the high point of Culture Club's career so far was the success of 'Karma Chameleon'. Months before it came out, George told an interviewer "It's got total Crosby, Stills, Nash and Young harmonies. It's really weird for us." Later he described it as his "Country and Western campfire song."

It sold over a million copies in three weeks. In Britain it won the Music Week Award as Top Single Of The Year, and did the same at the annual British Phonographic Industry Awards. It was Number One *everywhere*, and confirmed George's star status on the other side of the Atlantic.

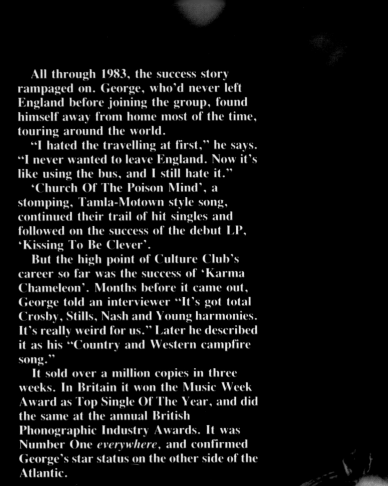

Seen as the spearhead of the second 'British Invasion' – a wave of young groups who are waking up the American music scene – George even appeared on the cover of Newsweek, pictured with Annie Lennox of Eurythmics who, with her penchant for male clothes, is often seen as George's female counterpart. Newsweek seemed at a loss to describe him, though. "Imagine a new wave Liberace," they suggested.

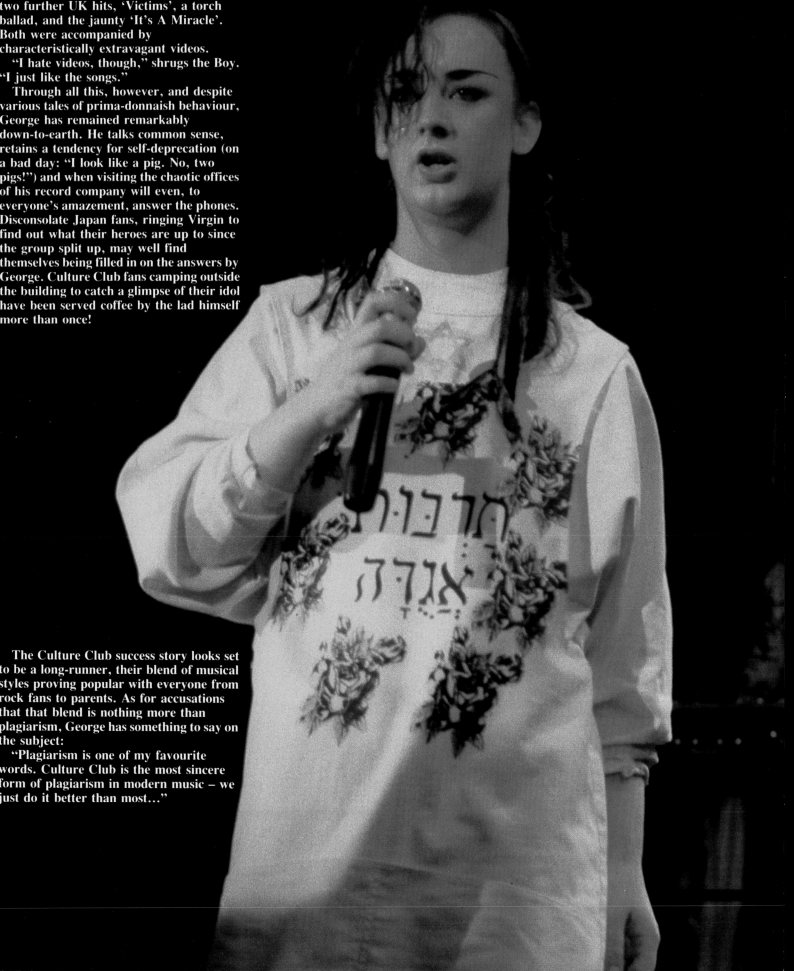

two further UK hits, 'Victims', a torch ballad, and the jaunty 'It's A Miracle'. Both were accompanied by characteristically extravagant videos.

"I hate videos, though," shrugs the Boy. "I just like the songs."

Through all this, however, and despite various tales of prima-donnaish behaviour, George has remained remarkably down-to-earth. He talks common sense, retains a tendency for self-deprecation (on a bad day: "I look like a pig. No, two pigs!") and when visiting the chaotic offices of his record company will even, to everyone's amazement, answer the phones. Disconsolate Japan fans, ringing Virgin to find out what their heroes are up to since the group split up, may well find themselves being filled in on the answers by George. Culture Club fans camping outside the building to catch a glimpse of their idol have been served coffee by the lad himself more than once!

The Culture Club success story looks set to be a long-runner, their blend of musical styles proving popular with everyone from rock fans to parents. As for accusations that that blend is nothing more than plagiarism, George has something to say on the subject:

"Plagiarism is one of my favourite words. Culture Club is the most sincere form of plagiarism in modern music – we just do it better than most…"

George has described Culture Club as his "family", and that's a pretty good description of the group's set-up. There's a nucleus group and the cousins, associate members if you like, like keyboard player and occasional co-writer Phil Pickett, singer Helen Terry and of course producer Steve Levine.

The atmosphere within the group is like a family, too – you may argue with your family, detest them at times, even, but in the end, blood is thicker than water.

Mikey and George can have dreadful slanging matches, and George and Jon's relationship, the most crucial within the group, has always been extremely volatile.

Jon Moss is the second most important member of Culture Club, however much they may dislike that sort of observation. From the beginning, he has tempered George's inexperience with his own hard-won knowledge of the music business, and matched his sound business sense with George's creativity to build their success.

Born on 11th October, 1957 to an unmarried Jewish girl from Middlesbrough, he was adopted by the Moss family, who named him Jonathan Aubrey, and was brought up in their well-heeled North London home.

He went to a London public school and studied up to 'A'Level, gaining passes in English, Politics and History, and a more than passing interest in playing the drums. Leaving school, he dabbled in various jobs both inside and outside the music business. His real involvement with the music scene, though, came with the punk era.

He enjoyed a brief stint on drums with the Clash in their early days, then left to form his own group, London. Whilst with London, a readers' poll in a teenage girls' magazine elected him "the prettiest punk", defeating such famous contemporaries as the Clash's Paul Simenon and Jean-Jacques Burnel of the Stranglers.

But London proved less popular. When they split up, Jon was enlisted into another big-name punk band, the Damned. Whilst within their ranks, on New Year's Eve 1977, Jon was involved in a car crash which left the prettiest punk with the scars you can still see today. None of the group came to see him in hospital.

Eventually, the Damned went the way of London, thought they were later to reform (without Jon). The heavy, doomy-sounding Edge were Jon's next band, but they weren't destined for fame either, and eventually changed their name and became the backing group for a singer called Jane Aire. It was hack work, really, and Jon hated it.

In the end, he left. Adam Ant called him in to play on a couple of songs, but the collaboration didn't last. Fed up with the seemingly endless disappointments of his musical career, Jon went to work for a West End video company. Then one day, George rang him and suggested he come and audition... and the rest is history.

As well as running the business side of the group in the early days, Jon proved able to impose a sort of discipline on George, in a very friendly way, both in making his behaviour a little calmer and in his work.

"My songs then were like art school poems," George remembers, "twenty paragraphs, pages and pages of words. Jon said 'Where's the chorus? Where's the beginning? Where's the ending?'" Their creative and personal friendship remains at the heart of the Culture Club family.

Mikey Craig had been the first to join up with George. Born Michael Emile Craig on 15 February 1960 in Hammersmith, he was a talented schoolboy footballer and claims to have turned down trials with both Fulham and Brentford football clubs. Like George, he began to frequent the London clubs as a teenager, but unlike George he seemed to have "settled down" by the time he was about sixteen.

He was living with his girlfriend Cleo then, Cleo being the daughter of Women's Aid founder Erin Pizzey and sister of Amos, a.k.a. 'Captain Crucial' who appeared as a guest member of the early Culture Club. Mikey and Cleo had two children while still in their mid-teens; a son named Kito and a daughter, Amber. (The couple have since separated, and Cleo and the children live in New Mexico.) Mikey worked as a labourer to support his young family.

They lived in Bristol for a couple of years. On his return to London, Mikey managed to impress George with his playing, which he'd been practising throughout his exile from the capital. Culture Club, though, was his first band.

The last member to be recruited was Roy Hay, who replaced the charmingly-named but musically inadequate Suede on guitar. He was recommended by one of George's Foundry customers, and proved to be, like Mikey, a talented musician who hadn't been through the mill of a dozen other groups – he was still young and fresh.

Born in Southend on 12 August 1961, Roy grew up in Essex and, on leaving school, enjoyed a rather more steady work record than the rest of Club colleagues. He worked for three years in an insurance office, then became a hairdresser. He learned to play his instrument in the privacy of his own bedroom, though he did play with one or two unknown local groups before meeting George.

He is the musician's musician within Culture Club; the music is *all* to him, and he's often seen to be bemused or even disapproving of the showbusiness paraphernalia and press sensation that inevitably surround the group.

"Culture Club is basically a song-writing and recording outfit," he says, "a band in the true sense of the word, but with a glamour boy. I hate the publicity side of it all. I think it's so unnecessary."

As the only married man in the group, Roy might appear in more ways than one to be the odd man out in Culture Club, but he

isn't really. Just one of the family.

"I suppose," George reflected at one time, "there's not much else you can do with the look. It defies the realms of sanity."

The look has been copied all over the world, by individual fans and by fashion companies. In the summer of 1983, Boy George hit the headlines when he stormed into a branch of Miss Selfridge to complain about "Culture Club rip-off" outfits displayed in their window. Sue Clowes, the designer who originated the Culture Club look, was eventually paid compensation by the embarrassed copycat manufacturers.

These days, however, George has moved on from Sue's work and generally wears clothes specially made for him by another young British designer, Dexter Wong. It was Dexter who first dressed George in the outsized shirt-and-tie look, and variations on that theme can be found at his London

shop, within the Hyper Hyper complex in Kensington, London.

George and Dexter work on the ideas together – for example, George bought a bed-cover decorated with numbers while in Spain, and took it home for Dexter to cut up and make costumes out of.

"At first the shopkeeper wouldn't sell it to me unless I bought the bed as well," George laughs, "and we were arguing for twenty minutes until I brought out this big wad of money. Then he shut up immediately and sold it."

The plaited locks which were such a big part of George's look when he first came to fame were in fact a fake. That's why he always wore a hat over them! He had a collection of different ones, attached to giant combs which he could fix into his own hair (which he was growing long) – then he'd jam the hat on top, and no-one would be any the wiser. Now, of course, his own hair is shoulder-length, and he sets it on huge heated rollers to get his curly look.

Though he often uses a make-up artist now, he's always been more than able to create a stunning make-up of his own.

"I enjoy dressing up and I enjoy collecting clothes," he says. "I enjoy make-up and the way it transforms me...Sometimes I get up in the morning and think, God you look so ugly, then I do myself up and I feel great."

Jewellery is another favourite means of ornamentation – as big and bold as possible. George's favourite jewellery designer is a young Londoner called Monty Don, whose work is also favoured by actress Joan Collins. If, for example, you've seen George pictured in an Egyptian-looking jewelled collar and matching armlets, they're Monty's work.

The Monty Don connection even led to a surprising link between the Boy and Mrs Margaret Thatcher. During 1984's British Fashion Week, the Prime Minister held a reception at 10 Downing Street for a number of British designers, Monty Don among them. She admired a brooch worn by one of the other guests, and when the designers wanted to send her a gift of thanks, they decided to ask Monty Don to recreate the brooch for Mrs Thatcher.

So Mrs Thatcher duly received her own metal Maltese cross brooch studded with crystal and hung on a blue ribbon...just like the one that Monty had already made for George!

In contrast to his extravagant costumes, George's feet are generally clad in sensible training shoes. On stage he goes barefoot, or wears an extraordinary variation on his trainers.

"The sports company Puma were pestering me to wear their shoes," he explains. "One day I was in this restaurant in Germany and I drew a pair of shoes on my serviette and said if they could make them, I'd wear them. I drew a sort of pair of platform running shoes but I never thought they'd do it – they were horrified! But they did – they turned up with them on the first day of our show, and Mikey and I wore them on stage."

George styles all the rest of the group, overseeing their own individual ideas. Occasionally he'll even run up outfits for them himself, as with the top he made for Mikey out of a string vest, cut up and put back together again and trimmed with beads and feathers. The eye-catching visors the group sometimes wear, covered in magazine cuttings, were George's creation too. He intends returning to the world of fashion, designing a range of clothes in the not-too-distant future, though what shape this project will take hasn't been decided. It may well be called "Common Currency", though you may rest assured that George's designs will be uncommon as ever.

What is underneath all George's finery, though? Part of the answer is provided by a friend who remembers watching George try on a new suit at the maker's, until instructed to turn around. "Turn round! You're not going to see me in me Y-fronts!"

The rest comes from George.

"I had one woman write and say 'I don't love my husband, I'm in love with you' I wrote back and said 'If you saw what was underneath the clothes, you wouldn't say that.'"

Although George's appeal is based on cheery charm rather than sex appeal, his make-up and clothes have led to a ravening

interest in his sexual preferences. He tends to dodge questions about homosexuality with quips like "Do I sleep with men? I try to stay awake, actually, whoever I'm in bed with."

Some of his more outrageous or dogmatic statements on the subject make a lot more sense when put in context. He has said "I'm not a poof" – meaning, 'I'm not an effete, stereotype gay with a limp wrist and affectedly feminine mannerisms'. On the other hand, he once declared "I'm a poof with muscles" – meaning, 'I'm feminine in some ways, but I'm a man underneath!'

In his own words, "I'm quite masculine in my own way. I think that's one of the things people find discomfiting, and that's a good thing. It keeps them guessing."

One thing George is dead set against is casual sex, particularly the way that pop stars can take advantage of their situation.

"I've got a very puritanical streak in me. My attitude to this lifestyle is quite clear. I never ever sleep with anyone on the road, no matter how attractive they are, male or female. A lot of my songs are based on relationships and situations I've got myself into which have been really heavy. But none of my relationships have been fickle, I've always had long relationships with people, never three-week jobs."

This attitude is George's own, mind you, not one that's been passed on to him or instilled in him at an early age. His family are Irish Catholics, but lapsed ones.

"My mother lost her faith early because she had a child by a man she wasn't married to, so she had to leave Ireland and come to England. She believes to be a good person you have to prove it yourself – it's not clutching rosaries or getting on your knees, it's doing something worthwhile. My mother runs an old people's home and in her own way she thinks she's close to God and I think that's a great mentality,"

George's "puritan streak" doesn't only apply to sex. He's no liberal in other matters; for example, he attended the

premiere of 'Brimstone and Treacle', the film which starred Police singer Sting as an evil young man who rapes a handicapped girl, and found the whole thing utterly distasteful. Others were enthusiastic, but "I'm sorry," said George, "It made me feel sick."

He'll occasionally drink white wine, but that's the extent of the stimulants he uses. He admits to using 'speed' (amphetamines) when he was younger, but now has no time for the chemical additives that flavour pop success for many musicians.

"When I'm working I get very tense if I think the people around me are using drugs," he says. "I don't like the people who work for us to take them, especially the people who do it to be hip. Maybe it's because I feel I've got natural drugs."

With those sorts of attitudes, it's hardly surprising that parents who at first were a bit stunned by George's appearance, now see him as a perfectly acceptable idol for their kids. At the root of his sensibility lies George's respect for other people, something he expects to find in return.

"When I was at school I didn't giggle when blokes said 'I screwed her'. I thought it was horrible. I won't have that sort of thing around me, it's just a question of respect for people," he says.

Above all, whatever his eccentricities, George's sincerity is self-evident, and that's the most appealing thing about him. Let him have the last word, as usual:

"I write from the heart, whether it's a love song or a giggly little pop song. I write from the way I feel and the way people affect me. My songs are really about the love of life."